my itty-bitty bio

Stephen Hawking

Published in the United States of America by Cherry Lake Publishing
Ann Arbor, Michigan
www.cherrylakepublishing.com

Reading Adviser: Marla Conn, MS, Ed, Literacy specialist, Read-Ability, Inc.
Book Designer: Jennifer Wahi
Illustrator: Jeff Bane

Photo Credits: ©Alex Mladek/Shutterstock, 5; ©Anneka/Shutterstock, 7; ©Imran's Photography/Shutterstock, 9; ©Billy Bob Bain/flickr, 11, 22; ©woodleywonderworks/flickr, 13; ©arindambanerjee/Shutterstock, 15; ©spatuletail/Shutterstock, 17; ©Library of Congress/Wikimedia/Public Domain, 19, 23; ©David Fowler/Shutterstock, 21; Jeff Bane, cover, 1, 8, 12, 16

Copyright ©2020 by Cherry Lake Publishing
All rights reserved. No part of this book may be reproduced or utilized in any form or by any means without written permission from the publisher.

Library of Congress Cataloging-in-Publication Data

Names: Sarantou, Katlin, author. | Bane, Jeff, 1957- illustrator.
Title: Stephen Hawking / by Katlin Sarantou ; illustrated by Jeff Bane.
Other titles: My itty-bitty bio.
Description: Ann Arbor, MI : Cherry Lake Publishing, [2019] | Series: My itty-bitty bio | Includes bibliographical references and index.
Identifiers: LCCN 2019004219| ISBN 9781534147034 (hardcover) | ISBN 9781534149892 (pbk.) | ISBN 9781534148468 (pdf) | ISBN 9781534151321 (hosted ebook)
Subjects: LCSH: Hawking, Stephen, 1942-2018--Juvenile literature. | Physicists--Great Britain--Biography--Juvenile literature. | Amyotrophic lateral sclerosis--Patients--Great Britain--Biography--Juvenile literature.
Classification: LCC QC16.H33 S27 2019 | DDC 530/.092 [B] --dc23
LC record available at https://lccn.loc.gov/2019004219

Printed in the United States of America
Corporate Graphics

table of contents

My Story 4

Timeline 22

Glossary 24

Index 24

About the author: Katlin Sarantou grew up in the cornfields of Ohio. She enjoys reading and dreaming of faraway places.

About the illustrator: Jeff Bane and his two business partners own a studio along the American River in Folsom, California, home of the 1849 Gold Rush. When Jeff's not sketching or illustrating for clients, he's either swimming or kayaking in the river to relax.

my story

I was born in England.
It was 1942.

My family valued learning.

My father wanted me to be a doctor.

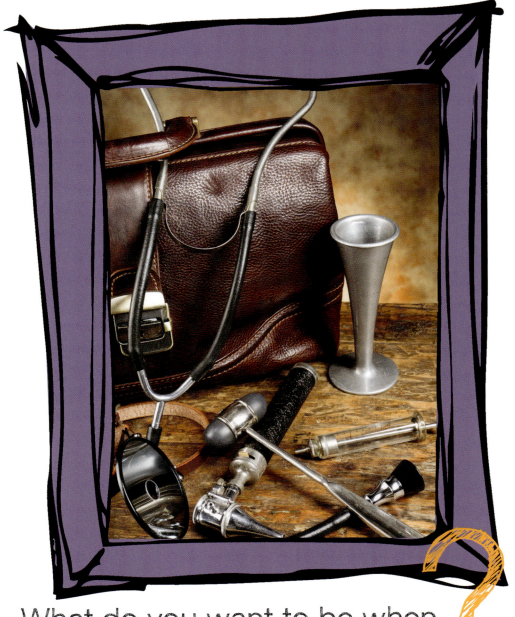

What do you want to be when you grow up?

I went to college.

I studied science.

I was **diagnosed** with **ALS**.

Doctors said I had 2 years to live. I was 21.

I didn't let ALS stop me. I lost my voice. But I still gave talks.

I helped design a machine that spoke for me.

What problem have you overcome?

I studied the universe. I wrote a book about its beginning.

I also studied **black holes**.

I discovered they give off **radiation**. This discovery is named after me.

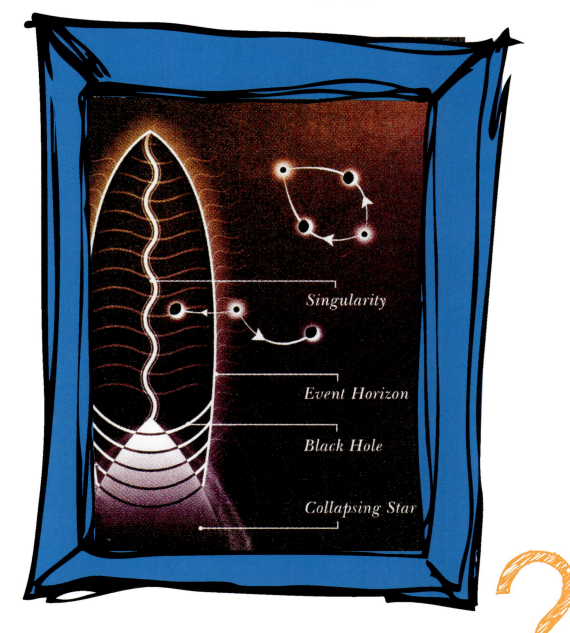

What's something you'd like to discover?

I made many **contributions** to science and physics.

I won awards. I won the **Presidential Medal of Freedom**.

I died peacefully in 2018. I was 76.

I **inspired** many scientists.

I changed the way people thought about the universe.

What would you like to ask me?

timeline

1963

1940

Born
1942

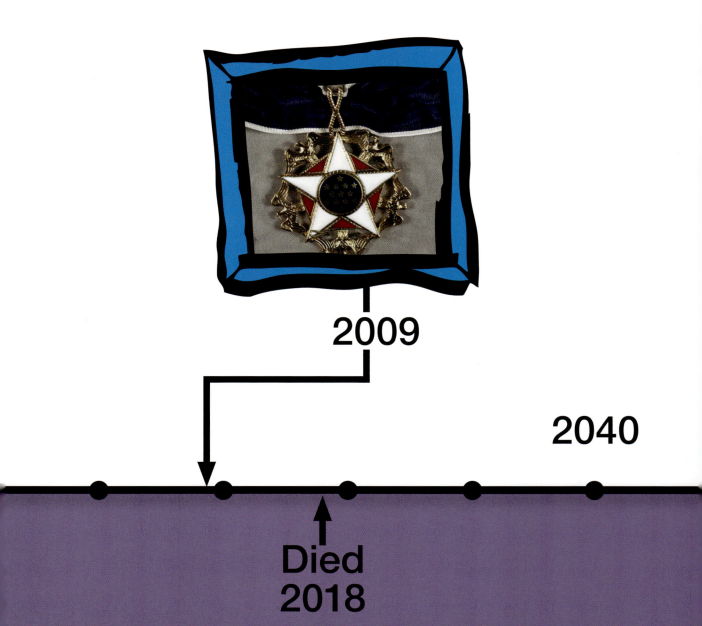

glossary & index

glossary

ALS (AY EL ES) a disease that causes muscle loss and the inability to move; also called Lou Gehrig's disease

black holes (BLAK HOHLZ) places in space where nothing, not even light, can escape

contributions (kahn-truh-BYOO-shuhnz) discoveries or advances in a field of study

diagnosed (dye-uhg-NOHSD) the act of identifying a disease

inspired (in-SPIRED) to feel the desire to do something

Presidential Medal of Freedom (prez-ih-DEN-shuhl MED-uhl UHV FREE-duhm) the highest award given to someone who is not in a military or police force

radiation (ray-dee-AY-shuhn) energy that comes from a source in the form of waves or rays you cannot see

index

ALS, 10, 12

black holes, 16
book, 14

England, 4

learning, 6

machine, 12

physics, 18
Presidential Medal of Freedom, 18

radiation, 16

science, 8, 18
study, 8, 14, 16

universe, 14, 20